A HANDBOOK ON

Death and Bereavement

Helping Children Understand

A HANDBOOK ON

Death and Bereavement

Helping Children Understand

COMPILED BY

Beverley Mathias
and
Desmond Spiers

National Library for the Handicapped Child
Reach Resource Centre

Published by the National Library for the Handicapped Child
Reach Resource Centre

Produced by Signpost Books 1992
Typeset by DP Photosetting, Aylesbury, Bucks
Printed by Risboro Printers Ltd, Princes Risborough, Bucks

ISBN 0 948664 10 X

The National Library for the Handicapped Child gratefully acknowledges the financial support of The John Spedan Lewis Foundation.

INTRODUCTION

This handbook came into being as a result of the considerable number of enquiries we receive from schools, therapists, and families for books which deal with death and bereavement. The areas that need to be covered appear to range from the sudden accidental death of a child to the death of a pet. Many of the enquirers were concerned about the effect death would have on a family, class group, friends, and acquaintances and wanted some indication of the ways in which worry, insecurity, and behavioural problems might show themselves.

On the surface, this does not appear to be a problem allied to reading, writing and language difficulties, but our experience has shown that, as with adults, this is probably one of the most severe disturbances a child will suffer. While the adult is expected to grieve and to go through a period of mourning, the child is often forgotten, not intentionally, but usually because it appears that the acceptance of death is immediate and then shrugged off. Children do suffer, and often they suffer more than is necessary because the adults around that child try to shield it from the more harrowing aspects of death, leaving the child's imagination to invent even more bizarre circumstances.

It is a known fact that when a family is separated through divorce, children will blame themselves and not their parents for the marriage breakdown. With the death of a parent or sibling, the child can attempt to take the blame, and may also try to shoulder responsibilities in place of the deceased parent or child.

For many children their first experience of death will be the loss of a pet. If it is an animal kept at school the teacher will probably help the children to mourn; there will be a small ceremony of burial, and the children will be encouraged to talk about the pet. A pet which lives at home is different. Parents can forget to inform the school, and the child mourns alone, often tearful, sometimes frustrated and indulging in violent or destructive behaviour.

While many children understand that death will come, and they do, in a way, expect grandparents to die, it is more difficult to face the death of a child, or a young adult. No matter how a child dies, through illness, incurable disease, accident or murder, the effect on those around that child is the same. Not only does the family have to deal with the loss, but also the child's school teacher, class mates, friends, community and religious groups, in fact anyone who has been even remotely connected with that child's life.

How can a teacher, parent, religious leader, librarian, social worker or other family or community member, help children and those around them come to terms with death?

To use books as bibliotherapy can be helpful, but it can also be too late — the worst has already happened. Preparing children for the fact of death removes it from their immediate experience, and while they might understand theoretically, nothing can prepare them for the finality of losing someone they love. The best approach is probably a combination of looking ahead, being prepared, and knowing where to go for help.

This handbook contains many titles, each of them dealing with death and bereavement. Some are picture books for small children, some picture books for older children. There are fiction titles for all age groups, and there are reference books for both children and adults. Some books are printed, some are on sound tape, some in large print, some are on video. The subjects covered include sudden accidental death, violent death, loss of parent, grandparent, sibling. Death through terminal illness of either a parent or a child is also included. Many of the books are difficult to read because of the emotions they bring forth. The whole purpose of the list is to show what is available, and to offer a representative collection of what we consider to be the best books about death and bereavement.

All available editions are listed including print and nonprint. This information was correct at the time of going to press, but as titles go out of print very quickly it is advisable to check before ordering. Some out-of-print titles have been included because they are important, and are probably available for loan through school or public library services. There are also a number of titles which are not published in Britain. These are available from UK booksellers, but some are very expensive.

As the situations in which the material might be used will range from the home and school to community and religious groups, it might be helpful to cite some of the enquiries we received, and the ways in which these have been answered.

1. A mainstream primary school returned from half term to face the death by drowning of a brother and sister. There were other members of the same family within the school.

The teachers were given information and lists of books which they could read quickly. The school was also supplied with a very brief list of picture books which could be read to the whole school in assembly. One of those books was about a child who drowned accidentally. Over a term, each class dealt with their grief openly, allowances being made for the family members, but care being taken that grieving and remorse never got out of control. At the end of the school year, a memorial assembly was held, the children talked of their friends, and a tree and bird bath were placed in the school grounds as a permanent memorial. The teachers are aware that certain activities and dates will continue to trigger a memory, and sometimes are able to comment before the situation arises.

2. Identical twin boys went home for the summer holidays. One developed incurable cancer and died just before the new school year began.

The school was given guidance and a list of books which dealt with similar situtations. The twin who returned was given support for as long as it was needed. His writing and reading suffered, he became introverted and needed time to work through his own grief.

3. A young mother, dying of cancer, asked the school and social services to help her find an adoptive home for her son, as she had no relatives.

With a list supplied by the NLHC, the class teacher spent time reading books about adoption, death, fostering and community care to the boy's class. They helped him put together a book about himself so that he had tangible memories of his natural mother. Because of the mother's courage, the boy was able to prepare himself in part for the loss of his parent, and the school was involved all the time, offering a stable environment to the child.

4. A six year old suffering from a respiratory complaint collapsed and died at home.

The class reacted by playing games about dying for almost a whole term. In that time, they read books about death, including pets and children, and explored through language and action what they understood about death, until they could distinguish between playing 'dead', and actually dying. The class teacher allowed the play to develop, while being constantly attuned to what the children were doing so that the maximum use and effect was gained without the time deteriorating into totally unstructured play.

The books contained in this listing cover many aspects of the same form of death. When a grandparent dies the child might be any age from infancy up, and the list reflects this. The guilt that some children feel at being left behind when a friend or sibling dies is also dealt with in a variety of ways. Non-attendance at school is also covered. Some children will refuse to return to school as they don't want to face their friends. A child finds it just as difficult as an adult to accept sympathy.

Among the books for adults are some that deal with how to explain death to children: the facts of death, burial, cremation and religious observances. Also included are books for teachers, care workers and community groups, which help work through the traumas, blame, guilt and relief which can both precede an expected death and follow a sudden death.

There are some exclusions from this list. Devotees of *Charlotte's Web* will notice that it is missing. This is because the death of Charlotte the spider is incidental in the development of Wilbur's character, and although essential to the story is not the main thrust. Where death is used as a vehicle to explain or allow the development of an ancillary plot the title has been excluded. However where a death allows a character to explore his or her own feelings in retrospect, that title is included.

The sheer quantity of material available means that some selection has had to be made and hopefully, this collection contains more than sufficient material to meet most needs. Because many of the children can't use print, we have included the book in other forms where possible.

A keyword indexing system has been used. Against each keyword are the numbers of the entries which apply to that particular topic. Some titles may be keyword indexed more than once. All books are listed by title, and there is an author index. The age interest level is only approximate, and it should be remembered that many of the titles can and should be used with a wide age range. A key to the age interest level is given on page 7.

The compilers would be delighted to receive note of titles which might be included in any future editions.

Beverley Mathias MA (Surrey) BA (Monash) ALAA
Desmond Spiers ALA

SOME SUGGESTIONS FOR USING THE HANDBOOK

The information in this handbook can be used as the basis for in-service training of teaching and ancillary staff, and where possible with the co-operation of a local counsellor in bereavement. Given sufficient notice, most public and school library services can provide a small exhibition of some of the titles so that these can be read before the seminar. Discussion amongst professionals is essential if the books are to be used wisely and to their best advantage. Some schools may wish to draw up their own list, using some of the information contained here, so that material outside the age range of the school can be excluded. THIS HANDBOOK MUST NOT BE PHOTOCOPIED

Where children use nonverbal communication methods, it might be best to concentrate on sound tapes (if applicable) and video. Some of the picture books included can be signed for use with children who use a signed language. Unfortunately no picture book about death is available in signed language. For children using braille it would be best to contact the child's school and the Royal National Institute for the Blind for information about braille editions of any of the books listed. Large print editions have been included, and a Kurtzweil reading machine, Opticon or Viewscan will read any print edition.

KEY TO ABBREVIATIONS OF EDITIONS

Hb — hardback
Pb — paperback
Lp — large print
Vid — video
Cas — sound cassette
Pam — pamphlet

KEY TO AGE INTEREST LEVELS

Ps Preschool
I Infant
Lp Lower primary
Up Upper primary
S Secondary
A Adult reference

1 AFTER THE FIRST DEATH

Cormier, Robert
Victor Gollancz, 1979, *0 575 02665 0* Hb
Lions, 1980, *0 00 671705 5* Pb
Windrush, 1988, *1 85089 905 3* Lp

A story of violent death through terrorism. A group of children travelling on a school bus are kidnapped. Each of the children, plus the young woman driver, must cope in their own way with the unstable mental condition of the young kidnappers. Ben/Mark, one of the victims on the bus, is writing the story as he waits for his mother to arrive on her annual visit to the military academy where he has been sent for his education. This is a raw and challenging story which asks the reader to take sides, to weigh loyalty for your country against family, and deceit against truth.

AGE INTEREST LEVEL: S

2 AFTER THE RAIN

Mazer, Norma Fox
Macmillan, 1988, *0 333 47203 9* Hb
Macmillan, 1989, *0 333 47204 7* Pb
Mammoth, 1991, *0 7497 0324 5* Pb
Chivers Press, 1989, *0 7451 0964 0* Lp

To begin with Rachel resented the time she was expected to spend visiting her grandfather. He was demanding and critical, and she felt nothing she did was appreciated. His deafness didn't help communication. When Rachel found out he was dying of cancer, she slowly began to build a relationship with the old man that took over her

previous peer group friendships and developed into an important part of her life. His slow death in hospital was something Rachel tolerated but couldn't come to terms with. It was instinct that made her defy her parents and stay with her grandfather the night he died. A moving story of the way a generation gap can assist teenagers to understand themselves and those around them.
AGE INTEREST LEVEL: S

3 THE ANATOMY OF BEREAVEMENT: A HANDBOOK FOR THE CARING PROFESSIONS

Raphael, Beverley
Unwin Hyman, 1990, *0 04 445362 0* Pb
By relating the findings of a number of pieces of research, and by presenting brief case studies, the author allows the reader to gain an insight into the ways people grieve and the various coping techniques they may employ. Two comprehensive chapters deal with the bereaved child and the adolescent's grief and mourning. The author attempts to show how children perceive death at different ages and how they respond and grieve.
AGE INTEREST LEVEL: A

4 ARE YOU LISTENING, KAREN?

Day, David
Andre Deutsch, 1983, *0 233 97537 3* Pb
Puffin, 1985, *0 14 031748 1* Pb
Karen is dead, but Jay needs to talk to her, to discuss the difficulties of growing up — in fact all the things he didn't have a chance to talk about because she died so suddenly. While he resents her going and mourns her, Jay also needs to explain and apologise for remembered hurts. He spends time sitting beside her grave talking to her in his head, telling her what has happened since she died. This is not a morbid book, but a realistic story of a young teenager trying to come to terms with the death of a much loved and respected older sister.
AGE INTEREST LEVEL: S

5 BEGINNINGS AND ENDINGS WITH LIFETIMES IN BETWEEN

Mellonie, Bryan
Ingpen, Robert
Dragons World, 1987, *1 85028 038* X Hb

This picture book was first published in Australia where it was received with acclaim. It sensitively shows that there is a beginning and an ending to everything with a time to live in between. The same applies to plants, insects, birds. fishes and animals as well as humans. Death is just another part of living.

AGE INTEREST LEVEL: Lp,Up

6 A BEGONIA FOR MISS APPLEBAUM

Zindel, Paul
Red Fox, 1991, *0 09 987210* 2 Pb
Bodley Head, 1989, *0 370 31268* 6 Pb

On their return to school Zelda and Henry discover that their favourite teacher has left. By asking questions and doing some guesswork they realise that Miss Applebaum is terminally ill. The two young people visit her at home and, enlivened by her failure to give up, proceed to help Miss Applebaum do what she wants to do with the time she has left. She opens their eyes and their minds to new experiences, encourages them to ask questions, and guides them through new emotions. Her death is in a way a victory, and although bereft, Zelda and Henry gain a lot from that three months packed with activity.

AGE INTEREST LEVEL: S

7 BOOKS TO HELP CHILDREN COPE WITH SEPARATION AND LOSS: AN ANNOTATED BIBLIOGRAPHY, VOL.3

Bernstein, Joanne & Rudman, Masha Kabakow
Bowker, 1988, *0 8352 2510 0* Hb

This American publication lists 600 annotated fiction and non-fiction titles which cover all aspects of separation and loss — leaving home, new school, moving house, foster care, adoption, divorce, war and displacement as well as death. Some ninety of the titles mentioned deal with death, and many of them have been published in this country.

AGE INTEREST LEVEL: A

8 BRIDGE TO TERABITHIA

Paterson, Katherine
Gollancz, 1978, *0 575 02550 6* Hb
Heinemann Educ, 1984, *0 435 12283 5* Hb
Puffin, 1986, *0 14 031260 9* Pb
Cornerstone, 1987, *1 55736 010 3* Lp

Lonely and unhappy, Jess makes friends with Leslie and together they visit a make-believe land called Terabithia, which in the real world is an island in a dry creek bed. In their own kingdom they are invincible and can put aside real life problems with siblings and school. Leslie's tragic death is a severe shock, but from it Jess learns many things about himself.

AGE INTEREST LEVEL: Up

9 BRIEF LIVES: Living with the death of a child

Foster, Suzanne and Smith, Pamela
Arlington Books, 1987, *0 851040 706 4* Pb

BRIEF LIVES: Living with the death of a child

Thames Television, nd, no ISBN, Pb

Together these books cover a television series which ran for six consecutive weeks. The book published by Thames gives an outline of the content for each programme, and includes a list of helpful names and addresses. The Arlington book is a series of articles and interviews with, by, and about families and professionals who are included in the series. Although it is helpful to have seen the programmes the books are a good introduction to a very painful subject. These children died by accident, through terminal illness, or violently at the hands of others. Their parents and families speak openly about the loss, anger, grief and sadness they felt and still experience.

AGE INTEREST LEVEL: A

10 CARE OF THE DYING

Lamerton, Richard
Penguin, 1988, rev ed *0 14 022275 8* Pb

The major part of this book deals with the time before death, when the adult or child is dying of a terminal illness, the result of an accident, etc. It looks at the various ways of caring and the people who can help: the hospice movement, social workers, doctors, family members and friends. Two chapters look at the right time to die, and euthanasia, both

very emotive subjects. Finally the author puts forward an explanation of what death might involve, and explores ways of coming to terms with grief.
AGE INTEREST LEVEL: A

11 CATHERINE

Dunbar, Maureen
Penguin, 1987, *0 14 008730 3* Pb
Penguin, 1990, *0 14 034223 0* Pb
Catherine Dunbar died of anorexia nervosa at the age of twenty-two. From the age of fifteen she systematically starved herself until she weighed less than 19 kilograms. She went through all the stages — refusing food, bingeing, worrying about weight gain, being dissatisfied with her looks, rejecting help. Her family suffered with her, and despite all attempts to help her overcome the illness, she was determined to die. While this is a very stark and sad story, it does point up the problems a family faces when one member becomes, to all intents and purposes, terminally ill.
AGE INTEREST LEVEL: S,A

12 CATHY'S STORY

Brighton, Catherine
Evans Brothers, 1980, *0 237 44969 2* Hb
While waiting at home one day for her mother, Cathy delivers letters to the other occupants of the building and is welcomed in by an old lady living upstairs. Together they explore a past childhood, and over the summer Cathy often visits the old lady to listen to her stories. Her mother reminds Cathy of events in their own lives which can be relived through memory. When the old lady dies, Cathy keeps the hat box of photographs as a reminder of the old lady and their shared moments.
AGE INTEREST LEVEL: I,Lp

13 THE CHARLIE BARBER TREATMENT

Lloyd, Carole
Julia MacRae, 1989, *0 86203 390 X* HB
Walker Books, 1990, *0 7445 1488 6* Pb
Simon is fifteen when he arrives home from school one day to find his mother dead on the floor. His way of coping is to clam up, and friends,

family and neighbours are given the cold shoulder. This carries on for six months until he meets Charlie Barber, who is staying with her grandmother for a week. She is a year older than Simon and he finds her fascinating. In their brief time together, he comes to accept his mother's death as he is able to talk about her with Charlie. Even his father is able to talk about his wife to Charlie. Her appearance is the catalyst to many emotions.

AGE INTEREST LEVEL: Up,S

14 CHILDREN, DEATH AND GRIEF

Musty, Erica
BFSS National Religious Centre
West London Institute Of Higher Education
Lancaster House
Borough Road
Isleworth
Middlesex TW7 5DU Pam

A twenty-four page booklet giving a brief introduction to the ways in which children react to and understand death. The author looks at how different age groups, infant, toddler, pre-school, school age and adolescent respond, and how they deal with the shock, denial, searching, despair, anger, anxiety and guilt that they go through. A section deals with the role of the school as a supportive caring agency in bereavement care.

AGE INTEREST LEVEL: A

15 CHINESE HANDCUFFS

Crutcher, Chris
Pan, 1991, *0 330 31314* 2 Pb

Preston, Dillon's brother, has committed suicide. Dillon's way of dealing with it is to immerse himself in competing in triathlons and becoming antagonistic to most of the world. In addition he is having difficulties with two girls — Preston's girlfriend and his own. They both have problems, and the latter is a victim of sexual abuse. Through writing letters to his dead brother and recording his memories of their time together as children, his envy, his hate and how he feels about the world in general, Dillon slowly gets rid of the guilt he feels over Preston's death.

AGE INTEREST LEVEL: S

16 COPING WITH BEREAVEMENT: COMING TO TERMS WITH A SENSE OF LOSS

Horn, Sandra

Thorsons, 1989, *0 7225 1651 7* Pb

Though bereavement is no longer the taboo subject it once was, and there are many support groups and organisations to which one can turn, in the long term you need to be able to sort out your feelings and problems on your own. This book contains pieces of information, thoughts, impressions and theories from people who have experienced bereavement, and those who have helped them. Fourteen chapters deal with such topics as attitudes to death, depression, the funeral, letting go and learning to live separately, children and bereavement, etc.

AGE INTEREST LEVEL: A

17 COPING WITH DEATH

Raab, Dr Robert A.

Rosen, 1989, *0 8239 0960 3* Hb

The author hopes that this book, which is aimed at the young adult, will enlighten rather than frighten, and that the reader will find fresh insights into the age-old problem of death and bereavement. Various chapters look at suicide, growing old, the cost of dying, the child and death, AIDS — what to do, etc. Each chapter is no longer than twenty pages and very easy to read. As this is an American publication some of the terms might need explaining.

AGE INTEREST LEVEL: S,A

18 THE COURAGE TO GRIEVE: Creative living, recovery and growth through grief

Tatelbaum, Judy

Cedar, 1986, *0 434 11105 8* Pb

The author charts the most common steps from the shock of death, through the varying ways in which we grieve to eventual acceptance of loss. She talks of having the courage to admit loss and allowing grief to happen. One chapter is devoted to the ways in which children face death and grief and offers suggestions as to how to help them through the experience. Unlike some writers and therapists Tatelbaum speaks of the 'rounding off' or 'finishing' of grief — coming to terms and allowing the dead to go and the living to continue life. An interesting and stimulating

study which should offer views for discussion in counselling courses and also help for the newly bereaved.
AGE INTEREST LEVEL: A

19 DEAD BIRDS SINGING

Talbert, Marc
Hamish Hamilton, 1986, *0 241 11770 4*, Hb
Puffin, 1988, *0 14 032184 5* Pb
In one second flat, Matt is deprived of his one parent and his sister. He wakes to find his mother dead and his sister so seriously injured she is not expected to live. His sister dies, and Matt moves in with friends to begin the slow pull back to normality. He fights with his best friend, becomes belligerent and uncooperative, but eventually is able to face his bitterness, and realise that his loss, although devastating, was a tragic accident.
AGE INTEREST LEVEL: S

20 DEATH AND BEREAVEMENT

Mental Health Media Council, 1991
380 Harrow Road
London W9 2HU Pam
This is a directory of films and videos that are available for sale or hire in the UK. The compilers state that 'it is not an evaluated or recommended list, but a starting point for a wide range of courses and seminars'.
AGE INTEREST LEVEL: A

21 DEATH AND DYING

Saunders, Pete
illustrated with photographs
Gloucester Press, 1990, *0 7496 0431 X* Hb
This book is one in the 'Let's Talk About' series which looks at topics young people are interested in and tries to answer the questions they ask. Questions raised in this book include: What has death got to do with me? What is death? What is a funeral for? Do people ever feel better after someone dies? Each question is dealt with in a two page spread and the text is complemented with excellent colour photographs.
AGE INTEREST LEVEL: Up,S

22 DEATH CUSTOMS

Mayled, Jon

Wayland, 1986, *0 85078 719 X* Hb

One of the 'Religious Topics' series, this book looks at the main religions of the world and their customs with regard to death. Each chapter, of three or four pages, is accompanied by colour photographs which help convey some of the emotions and feelings that can be expressed.

AGE INTEREST LEVEL: Up,S

23 DEATH IN WORLD RELIGIONS

Musty, Erica

BFSS National Religious Education Centre
West London Institute of Higher Education
Lancaster House
Borough Road
Isleworth
Middlesex TW7 5DU Pam

A look at how the main world religions — Christianity, Sikhism, Islam, Hinduism, Judaism, Buddhism — deal with death and also Humanism. This is a brief and very readable introduction.

AGE INTEREST LEVEL: A

24 THE DEATH OF A CHILD: A BOOK FOR FAMILIES

Wilkinson, Tessa

Rowe, Gavin

Julia MacRae, 1991, *1 85681 250 2* Pb

The author is a bereavement counsellor for the Helen House Hospice, and has written this book in response to numerous requests for help to cope with the death of a child, not just from the adult point of view, but also from the point of view of other children in the family. The book has been divided into two parts: the first gives practical and helpful advice for adults, and the second is a picture story about death that can be read and shared with children.

AGE INTEREST LEVEL: A

25 DEATH RITES

Pictorial Charts Educational Trust
27 Kirchen Road
London W13 0UD

This is the final set of charts in the series 'Rites of Passage'. The charts illustrate three religions — Christian, Sikh and Buddhist, and the fourth chart shows the death rites of the Chinese. A set of teachers' notes gives more information and in addition describe Jewish, Islamic and Hindu death rites.

AGE INTEREST LEVEL: S,A

26 DEATH: THE FINAL JOURNEY

Smith, Linda
Lion Publishing, 1990, *0 7459 1336 9* Pb

'Miss, isn't it stupid that we spend all this time on Maths and French and stuff but nobody teaches you what to do about death'. This quotation from a fifteen-year-old boy whose sister had been knocked off her bicycle and killed sums up the purpose of this book. It is primarily aimed at teachers who wish to look at the subject in the class room. The book starts with the personal and then works through the social, moral, and religious dimensions of the subject. Though it mainly deals with the Christian viewpoint other religions are brought in.

AGE INTEREST LEVEL; S,A

27 THE DIDDAKOI

Godden, Rumer
Pan/Macmillan, 1991, *0 30 32397 0* Pb
Chivers, Cas

Kizzy is a Diddakoi — a half-gypsy. Though she is bullied and teased at school she copes as she has her gran, Joe the horse and the caravan. When Gran dies her world is turned upside down, and she has to come to terms not just with her grief, but the loss of the life style to which she has become accustomed. The social services move her into an 'ordinary' house, and she finds it difficult to cope with the restrictions.

AGE INTEREST LEVEL: Up,S

28 DOUBLE VISION

Wright, Gilli

Collins Lion, 1989, *0 00 672891 X* Pb

Sam is convinced he was responsible for his father's death and incarcerates himself in the flat, refusing to go to school or even to go out to shop. With his mother's birthday gift of binoculars, he begins to watch the houses on the hill opposite the tower block where he lives. He fantasizes about the people he sees, while still resisting the attempts of his mother and home teacher to go out into the world. Gradually, his interest in the people he observes overcomes his reluctance to leave the flat. Eventually, fact and fiction merge in his mind until Sam faces the reality of his father's death.

AGE INTEREST LEVEL: Up,S

29 EMMA SAYS GOODBYE

Nystrom, Carolyn

Large, Annabel

Lion, 1990, *0 7459 1608 2* Hb

Emma and her family watch helplessly as her Auntie Sue struggles against cancer. They see the agony of the chemotherapy treatment and the frustration as the cancer invades and takes over Auntie Sue's life. Emma is frightened and resentful as Auntie Sue becomes weaker by the day. The progression of the illness is marked by the making of a patchwork quilt. A quiet book which evokes emotion through family love and a strong religious conviction.

AGE INTEREST LEVEL: Lp,Up

30 EMMA'S CAT DIES

Snell, Nigel

Hamish Hamilton, 1984, *0 241 11297 4* Hb

For many children the death of a pet is their first experience of mortality. Emma has a cat called Simon whom she loves very much. One night Simon doesn't come in for his supper, and later Emma is told that the cat has been run over and killed. Emma bursts into tears but remembering the good times helps her to come to terms with her loss.

AGE INTEREST LEVEL: Ps,I

31 ENDS OR BEGINNINGS

Barnett, Vida

illustrated with photographs

Christian Education Movement, nd, *0 905022 87 2* Pb

A look at the important stages in a person's life — birth, baptism/naming ceremonies, marriage and death, as seen through various religions. Photographs complement the text.

AGE INTEREST LEVEL: S,A

32 FACING DEATH: Families and professionals

Stedeford, Averil

Heinemann, 1984, *0 433 31550 4* Pb

This book faces facts clearly and without compromise. It suggests that a final illness can be a period of growth for the family, including the one who is dying. Death is never easy, but talking and planning can help. The psychological barriers placed in the way by custom and fear can be overcome with care and support. Stress can be managed so that the inevitable death is seen as a continuum in the growth and nuture of the family. Because this is for professionals as well as families there is much that can be used as counselling support.

AGE INTEREST LEVEL: A

33 FACING GRIEF: BEREAVEMENT AND THE YOUNG ADULT

Wallbank, Susan

Lutterworth Press, 1991, *0 7188 2807 0* Pb

A guide to death and bereavement aimed specifically at the 18–28 age group. This is the time when most young adults leave home, start a career, and develop new relationships, all of which put pressure on them. The death of a friend or relative can be quite devastating. Divided into short chapters, this book deals predominantly with the practicalities of family deaths, including grieving, and emotional responses. A list of care groups and organisations who can be of help is given.

AGE INTEREST LEVEL: A

34 FAMILY

Hill, Susan

Michael Joseph, 1989, *0 7181 3169 X* Hb

Penguin, 1990, *014 010886* 6 Pb

Susan Hill has chronicled her experiences in trying to have a second child. She talks about the miscarriages she suffered, the lost children, and Imogen who died aged five weeks. Her own suffering is very evident, but she discusses too, the way in which her first daughter was affected while Susan and her husband were grieving for Imogen. While the book is partly about the death of an infant, it is also about the indignities and insensitivity suffered by women who have miscarriages or whose babies die prenatally.

AGE INTEREST LEVEL: A

35 FEELINGS

Aliki

Bodley Head, 1985, *0 370 30836 0* Hb

Pan Books, 1987, *0 330 29408 3* Pb

An illustrated comic-style book about emotions, showing the ways in which we communicate through words, gestures, and body language. One page depicts a conversation between two children about the death of a pet mouse.

AGE INTEREST LEVEL: I,Lp,Up

36 FIVE AND A HALF TIMES THREE: The short life and death of Joe Buffalo Stuart

Stuart, Alexander and Totterdell, Ann

Hamish Hamilton, 1990, *0 241 12889 7* Hb

Vintage, 1991, *0 09 98830 9* Pb

Joe died, aged five-and-a-half of a rare form of cancer. Into his short life his parents managed to pack a lot of living and loving. Through Joe's illness, they learnt about the way terminally ill children are treated by medical professionals. They questioned certain practices, and looked objectively and critically at the whole question of the care of the terminally ill child. Joe and his father wrote a book together which was published in the Hamish Hamilton Antelope series (*Henry and the Sea*). His parents documented and photographed the progression of Joe's illness, bravely recording not only the treatment but also their own

emotions. The end is extremely moving, showing their feelings at the moment of Joe's death and the short period afterwards very clearly.
AGE INTEREST LEVEL: A

37 FLOWERS FOR SAMANTHA

Parr, Letitia
Mullins, Patricia
Methuen, 1975, *0 454 00018 9* Hb
Samantha is the Tompkins family's pet cat. She is killed by a car, and the family share their grief, helping Katie, the youngest child, to come to terms with the loss of her friend. They remember all the good, funny, annoying and irritating things about Samantha as they prepare to bury her. They hold a quiet funeral and think about their much loved cat.
AGE INTEREST LEVEL: I

38 FREDDIE: A DIARY OF A COT DEATH

Key, Sarah
William Heinemann, 1991, *0 434 38370 8* Hb
The author writes about the cot death of her ten-week-old son. The account is very frank and honest. She was prompted to write this account of her grieving, because of the attitudes of family and friends. At the mention of his name people would clam up, and she felt that even his memory was going to have to be erased. She was also surprised at how little the professionals had to offer in the way of help in the grieving process.
AGE INTEREST LEVEL: A

39 FRIEDRICH

Richter, Hans Peter
Heinemann, 1978, *0 435 12226 6* Hb
Puffin, 1987, *0 14 032205 1* Pb
A classic story of life in Nazi Germany before and during the Second World War telling of the destruction of one Jewish family. The story is told through the eyes of a non-Jewish boy who was a friend of Friedrich. A harrowing account of man's inhumanity to man.
AGE INTEREST LEVEL: S

40 FUNERALS: and how to improve them

Walter, Dr Tony

Hodder and Stoughton, 1990, 0 340 53125 8 Pb

For most people, the question of arranging a funeral is something not even thought about until the need arises. Dr Walter writes with ease and in a matter-of-fact style about burial, cremation and funerals in general. He offers advice on religious and non-religious ceremonies, how the law affects the manner of a funeral, and what choices are available. The delicate matter of stillbirths, abortions and early infant death are discussed with sympathy. A list of helpful organisations is given along with a checklist to help anyone faced with having to arrange a funeral.

AGE INTEREST LEVEL: A

41 GIVE SORROW WORDS; WORKING WITH A DYING CHILD

Judd, Dorothy

Free Association Books, 1989, 1 85343 098 6 Pb

The author is a Kleinian psychotherapist who works with ill, disabled and dying children. Here she writes about her experiences in the context of new developments in hospice and hospital care. In the first third of the book, she looks at death and children generally — how people feel when a child dies, and children's attitudes to death. She then discusses the work that she did with a seven-and-a-half-year-old boy and his parents during the last three months of his life. The final section includes a chapter on whether life should be prolonged indefinitely.

AGE INTEREST LEVEL: A

42 GOODBYE, MAX

Keller, Holly

Julia MacRae, 1987, *0 86203 307 1* Hb

Walker Books, 1990, *0 7445 1455 X* Pb

Ben grieves for his old dog Max, and rejects the new puppy his parents bring home. His mother reminds him of the day Max died, of how old he was, and how the vet tried to help. As Ben and his friend Zach deliver papers, they remember some of Max's exploits, and console each other. A very simple text which is sympathetic to a child's grief.

AGE INTEREST LEVEL: Lp

43 GOODBYE RUNE

Kaldhol, Marit
Oyen, Wenche
Kane/Miller, 1987, *0 916291 11 1* Hb

One of very few books about the accidental drowning of a young child. The illustrations are muted, the text is thoughtful, sympathetic and factual without being cloying. Rune's friend wants to know if he will realise he is in a coffin, if he will grow older as she does, if he will ever return. She joins with the small community as they mourn the loss of the child, and leaves flowers on his newly dug grave.

AGE INTEREST LEVEL: I,Lp,Up

44 GOOD GRIEF
Volume One: Talking and learning about loss and death
GOOD GRIEF
Volume Two: Exploring feelings, loss and death with under 11's

Ward, Barbara and Houghton, James
Good Grief (1), 1988, *0 9512888 1 4* Pb
Good Grief (2), 1989, *0 9512888 2 2* Pb
Good Grief, 19 Bawtree Road, Uxbridge, Middlesex UB8 1PT
(new edition 1992)

An excellent two-volume work specially written for use in schools. The material is simple, clear, straightforward, and easily usable by a teacher prepared to do a little work beforehand. A number of topics are suggested for group discussion without needing to be linked to a specific incident. Much of the material can be freely photocopied, allowing a teacher to prepare additional material to support the basic lesson plan given. The subject of death is one which most teachers avoid unless dealing obliquely with the death of a pet. Here, for the first time, is something which can be part of normal teaching.

AGE INTEREST LEVEL: A

45 GRANPA

Burningham, John
Jonathan Cape, 1984, *0 224 02279 2* Hb
Jonathan Cape, 1989, *0 224 02731 X* Pb
Red Fox, 1990, *0 09 975240 9* Pb
Puffin, 1988, *0 14 050841 4* Pb
Palace, 1989, *PVC4036A* Vid

A two-level conversation runs through this lovely picture book as Granpa and his un-named granddaughter share days out and quiet times in the garden. Few children miss the significance of the empty chair, and most will talk about their own grandparents whether alive or dead. This is a quiet and sympathetic way to introduce quite young children to the mortality of even the most loved members of the family. The video includes dialogue which is not exactly the same as the written text.

AGE INTEREST LEVEL: Ps,I

46 GRANDPA'S SLIDE SHOW

Gould, Deborah
Harness, Cheryl
Viking Kestrel, 1989, *0 670 82232 9* Hb
Puffin, 1991, *0 14 050871 6* Pb

Sam and Douglas love their grandpa very much, and look forward to the slides he shows them of themselves and other members of the family. They learn to handle the remote control device and feel important as they help with the show. When their beloved grandpa dies, the boys miss him very much. They have difficulty understanding the traditions surrounding death: the funeral, the after-funeral party, all the relatives very subdued. They remember Grandpa in the way they know best, by assembling the projector and the slides and putting on a show for Grandma.

AGE INTEREST LEVEL: I,Lp

47 GRAN'S GRAVE

Green, Wendy
Benton, Ruth
Lion Publishing, 1989, *0 7324 0036 8* Pb

John holds a funeral for Spice, his dead gerbil. When his grandad comes for dinner, John tells him what has happened, which leads into a discussion about his dead grandmother. Together they visit Gran's grave and talk about the memories they have of her.

AGE INTEREST LEVEL: Lp

48 GRIEF — A Play

Casdagli, Penny

Neti Neti Theatre Co. 1991 *0 9514242 1 3* Pb

Performance Video, 1992

This is the script and video of a play about loss and bereavement among young people and its relationship to disruptive behaviour. The play is multilingual, being performed in English, British Sign Language and Bengali. Eddie and Amy are twins, and Eddie's sudden death has a powerful effect on Amy and their friends. She finds passionate and physically dangerous ways to express her grief, before realising there are many kinds of loss and the process of mourning, no matter how painful, can lead to change. The book also contains writings from young people about their experiences of loss.

AGE INTEREST LEVEL: S,A

49 GRIEF IN CHILDREN: A HANDBOOK FOR ADULTS

Dyregrov, Atle

Jessica Kingsley, 1991, *1 85302 113 X* Pb

This handbook explains children's understanding of death at different ages, and gives detailed outlines of exactly how adults can best help them cope with the death, whether it is of a parent or sibling, a relation or friend, a class mate or teacher. The book deals with a whole range of responses, from those on the physical and pragmatic level to psychological reactions which may be less obvious to the caring adult.

AGE INTEREST LEVEL: A

50 HELPING CHILDREN COPE WITH GRIEF: Facing a death in the family

Wells, Rosemary

Sheldon Press, 1989, *0 85969 559 X* Pb

For anyone faced with helping a child to come to terms with death — parents, friends, teachers, hospital and support staff, and religious leaders — this book offers sensible advice. It covers terminal illness, sudden accidental death, cot death, and the death of a child with a disablity. There are statements from children and young people as well as comments from adult family members. Teachers discuss how they dealt with the death of a classmate or the sibling of a class member. Wells points out how children can appear callous and unfeeling when in fact they are as deeply hurt as their parents. This is an extremely readable book which should be particularly useful to teachers and families.

AGE INTEREST LEVEL: A

51 HERE AND NEVER

Harley, Rex

Gollancz, 1990, *0 575 04754 2* Hb

Alice has succesfully blocked out her friend's suicide. To try and help Alice to remember, her mother sends her to stay with an old friend, Max, an artist. Alice meets some of the local people, and becomes very friendly with a boy. As their friendship develops, Alice finds herself talking about death with Max until her mother believes the time has come for Alice to face the missing period in her life. Alice finds herself able to continue her diary and writes down what actually happened on the day Chris took his own life and tried to take hers as well. This is not easy to read, as the reader is left in the dark with Alice until well into the story. It is, however, a good example of mind-blocking trauma which could be useful with teenagers.

AGE INTEREST LEVEL: S

52 HOW IT FEELS WHEN A PARENT DIES

Krementz, Jill

Illustrated with photographs

Victor Gollancz, 1983, *0 575 03290 1* Hb

Victor Gollancz, 1991, *0 575 05183 3* Pb

Jill Krementz is a photographer. She has interviewed and photographed a number of children of varying ages in order to present something that catches the essence of each child in text and picture. The children talk about the death of a parent, and many speak of the frustration of not being given enough information about the illness or manner of death. In some cases the remaining parent has remarried, so the children also give some insight into becoming part of a new family. This is a valuable resource to use with groups of children for general discussion, as well as with individuals.

AGE INTEREST LEVEL: Up,S

53 I DON'T KNOW WHAT TO SAY: HOW TO HELP AND SUPPORT SOMEONE WHO IS DYING

Buckman, Dr Robert

Macmillan, 1990, (rev ed) *0 333 54035 2* Pb

ISIS, 1989, *1 85089 335 7* Lp

The author states that he wrote this book 'for myself, and for anybody else who wants to but doesn't know how to help a friend or relative facing the end of his life'. The book has two main themes, firstly to explain the process of dying in enough detail to demystify it, and secondly to give practical advice to those who want to help. The majority of the text deals with adults, but there is plenty of information on how to cope with the death of a child, whether it be a son/daughter or sibling.

AGE INTEREST LEVEL: A

54 I HAD A FRIEND NAMED PETER: Talking to children about the death of a friend

Cohn, Janice

Owens, Gail

William Morrow, 1987, *0 688 06685 2* Hb (USA)

The introduction to this book details some of the questions a young child might ask about death, and offers ways of dealing with them. The story is about Betsy and her friend Peter, with whom she plays frequently. He is hit by a car and killed. Betsy's parents help her to grasp the finality of death: she is told about the funeral and burial and given the opportunity to decide if she wants to attend. At school, her teacher talks about Peter and they discuss him as a friend. This is a book which needs to be used either on a one-to-one basis or with a very small group. It is an excellent support for a teacher and class facing the sudden death of one of their group.

AGE INTEREST LEVEL: I,Lp

55 I'LL ALWAYS LOVE YOU

Wilhelm, Hans
Hodder and Stoughton, 1985, *0 340 38612 6* Hb
Knight Books, 1986, *0 340 40153 2* Pb

Elfie and the boy grow up together, sharing their joys and troubles. As the boy grows taller, Elfie the dog grows rounder and less able to romp and play. The family take Elfie to the vet, but age is taking its toll, and the boy has to face the fact that Elfie is getting old. Eventually, despite all the loving, Elfie dies peacefully in her sleep and is buried with due reverence by the family. A calm and gentle story of the love between a boy and his dog, which would do much to reassure a child who has recently suffered the death of a pet.

AGE INTEREST LEVEL: I,Lp

56 I'LL MISS YOU, MR. HOOPER

Stiles, Norman
based on his television script for Sesame Street
Mathieu, Joe
Random House, 1984, *0 394 86600 2* Hb

Using Big Bird to ask the questions, the human cast of Sesame Street help children to come to terms with the death of Will Lee who played Mr Hooper in the television series. Big Bird wants to give Mr Hooper a picture, and can't understand why this isn't possible. The cast help Big Bird to remember all the good things about Mr Hooper, explaining that you don't have to stop loving someone when they die.

AGE INTEREST LEVEL: I,Lp

57 ISAAC CAMPION

Howker, Janni
Julia MacRae, 1986, *0 86203 270 9* Hb
Heinemann Educ., 1988, *0 435 12326 2* Hb
Collins Lion, 1987, *0 00 672790 5* Pb

The feud between the two families began with the accidental death of a boy and continued over three generations. Knowing he is soon to die the old man who, as a young boy, witnessed that accidental death attempts to set the record straight by recounting what he saw and remembered. Detailed and intertwined with his account of the story are the death and bereavement customs of the time between two world wars, and the

superstitions and antagonisms within the small community. The bitterness and pain the old man feels is slowly overcome as Isaac makes decisions about his own life, irrespective of his deceased father's feelings and the long standing conflict between the two families.
AGE INTEREST LEVEL: S

58 THE KINGDOM BY THE SEA

Westall, Robert
Methuen, 1991, *0 416 15662 2* Hb
Chivers Press, 1991, *0 7451 1429 6* Lp
Mammoth, 1992, *0 7497 0796 8* Pb
Harry lives on Tyneside. The story is set during the Second World War and opens with a bombing raid by the Germans. Harry counts — a superstitious action: if you reach ten the bombs have missed you — but the last thing he remembers saying is seven. Harry survives, but his parents are killed. He decides to leave home as he doesn't want to be fussed over, and so begin his adventures on the road meeting people who have also been affected by the war — families split, relatives killed — all of whom help him come to terms with his loss. He is also able to give support to some of those who help him.
AGE INTEREST LEVEL: Up

59 KIRSTY'S KITE

Stilz, Carol Curtis
Harrison, Gwen
Lion Publishing, 1988, *0 7459 1494 2* Hb
Kirsty's mother has died, and she now lives with her grandfather as her father is at sea. She loves watching the kites being flown on the beach, and wishes she were a kite as she could then fly up to heaven and see her mum. With grandad she buys a kite, and he teaches her how to fly it just as he taught her mum when was a little girl. She talks to grandad about her mum's death and one day decides to lets the kite go so it can fly to heaven the way her mum did. With this symbolic gesture she finally accepts her mother's death.
AGE INTEREST LEVEL: Lp

60 LAST THINGS: SOCIAL WORK WITH THE DYING AND BEREAVED

Philpot, Terry (ed)

Reed Business, 1989, *0 617 01009* 9 Pb

Chapters in this book include Working With Bereaved Families, Teamwork in the Community, Setting Up and Running a Bereavement Service, The Future of the Hospice, The Dying Child, Bereavement and Mentally Handicapped People. Though this book aims to assist social workers play their part in helping people over a death and the grieving process, it will also be of use to teachers and any other professionals working with children and young adults.

AGE INTEREST LEVEL: A

61 LEILA

Alexander, Sue

Lemoine, Georges

Hamish Hamilton, 1986, *0 241 12265 1* Hb

Leila's brother Hamed has been lost from their Bedouin encampment in the desert and she is devastated. Her father decrees that Hamid's name must never be spoken again so that he cannot be reminded of what he has lost. Leila refuses to obey as she realises that without talking about Hamid she will lose him again, and this time for good. This picture book for the older reader is filled with evocative illustrations which extend the text in portraying Leila's unhappiness.

AGE INTEREST LEVEL: Up,S

62 LISTEN. MY CHILD HAS A LOT OF LIVING TO DO: CARING FOR CHILDREN WITH LIFE-THREATENING CONDITIONS

Baum, J. D. et al

Oxford University Press, 1990, *0 19 261898* 9 Hb

Oxford University Press, 1990, *0 19 261961* 6 Pb

Though death is not the main emphasis in this book, it has been included because of the authors' understanding of the care that children require and how important the role is between parents and professionals. Key ideas relevant to families and professional carers alike, run throughout the book — the loneliness, and the need to listen and communicate especially with other children in the family. With understanding, the family can cope with the situation in a much better way. Simply by knowing about the illness and its eventual sad outcome the death may not come as such a shock.

AGE INTEREST LEVEL: A

63 LITTLE OBIE AND THE FLOOD

Waddell, Martin
Lennox, Elsie
Walker Books, 1991, *0 7445 1902 0* Hb
Walker Books, 1991, *0 7445 1768 0* Pb

Set in the American West, this story tells how Marty came to live with Obie and his grandparents after her parents had been killed in a flood. It is not an easy time for any of them — trying to scrape a living while adjusting to their new family situation.

AGE INTEREST LEVEL: Lp,Up

64 LIVING WITH DEATH AND DYING

Kubler-Ross, Elisabeth
Souvenir, 1987, *0 285 64957 4* Pb

The author is a well-known psychiatrist specialising in work with the terminally ill. This book was written in response to the questions asked by patients, parents of terminally ill children, and people who had attended the author's workshops and seminars. Anecdotal in content and style, it contains four articles on different aspects of death and bereavement — talking to patients, sudden death, caring for a dying child and the way in which drawing pictures can help in times of stress.

AGE INTEREST LEVEL: A

65 THE MAGIC MOTH

Lee, Virginia
Cuffari, Richard
Longman Young, 1973, *0 582 16472 9* Hb

Maryanne is terminally ill with a heart defect. She is ten, her younger brother six. Mark-O doesn't understand why Maryanne won't get better, and continues to hope for her recovery. This is direct, honest and unsentimental, showing how one family tries to cope with its grief, and to support each other, especially the youngest child. At the moment of Maryanne's death a moth flies out of the window and this becomes a symbol for Mark-O to hold onto as he comes to terms with the loss of a much loved sister. The children all go to the funeral, including the burial; each one seeing it in a slightly different way, but combining as a family in their grief. Because of the emotion it evokes this is a difficult story to read.

AGE INTEREST LEVEL: Up

66 MAMA'S GOING TO BUY YOU A MOCKINGBIRD

Little, Jean

Puffin, 1986, *0 14 031737 6* Pb

When their father becomes ill, Jeremy and Sarah are sent to stay with their aunt. The story is mainly about Jeremy, although Sarah is evident in a minor way. When Jeremy and Sarah return home Jeremy realises his father is not going to recover and he has to face the death of his beloved parent. Looking for someone to talk to he remembers Tess, a girl from school who lives with her grandfather, and together they come to terms with their individual losses. A sensitive and moving story.

AGE INTEREST LEVEL: Up,S

67 MARY AND HER GRANDMOTHER

Egger, Bettina

Jucker, Sita

Viking, 1987, *0 670 81746 5* Pb

After a family funeral it is very easy to ignore or disregard the needs of children. Adults understand the grieving process but sometimes fail to see that children need this too. Mary and her parents grieve for her grandmother together, talking about the good times, remembering the things shared, and building a total picture of a much loved family member. They help her to come to terms with her grief and to understand the physical permanence of death while still holding onto memories.

AGE INTEREST LEVEL: I,Lp

68 MEETINGS AT THE EDGE: DIALOGUES WITH THE GRIEVING AND THE DYING, THE HEALING AND THE HEALED

Levine, Stephen

Anchor Books, 1984, *0 385 26221 3* Pb

Twenty-three conversations that the author had with people who were either dying or had experienced a death in the family. These include Dorothy, mother of a dying child; Karen, mother of a drowned child; Tom, son of a dying father. As the author states 'this may not be an easy book to read. It explores the fear and doubt, the courage and determination which arise in turn to confront the uncontrollable.'

AGE INTEREST LEVEL: A

69 MEMORY

Mahy, Margaret

Dent, 1987, *0 460 06269 7* Hb

Macmillan Educ, 1990, *0 333 49646 9* Hb

Puffin, 1988, *0 14 032680 4* Pb

Windrush, 1988. *1 85089 946 0* Lp

Jonny's sister is dead, nobody talks about her, and he feels that in some way it was his fault, even though he can't remember the accident clearly. He sets out to find his sister's closest friend and meets Sophie who has senile dementia and remembers nothing. His sister's friends shun him, not wanting to talk about the tragedy, but Sophie allows him to talk even though she barely understands what he says. There is humour and sadness in the way Sophie and Jonny help each other. Finally Jonny can face and understand what happened to his sister.

AGE INTEREST LEVEL: S

70 MY BROTHER STEALING SECOND

Naughton, Jim

Horizions, 1991, *0 330 31987 6* Pb

Billy was killed driving the car which also killed two others in the same accident. His brother Bobby feels that everything in his life has changed; he knows he is in a mess, but does it really matter anymore? Getting to know Annie Durham, whose parents were killed in the same car accident and who initially hates him for who he is, Bobby slowly comes

to terms with his grief. With Annie he finds out that the accident is not what it had seemed to be.
AGE INTEREST LEVEL: S

71 NANA UPSTAIRS & NANA DOWNSTAIRS

DePaola, Tomie
Methuen, 1987, *0 416 43070 8* Hb
A fortunate young boy has a grandmother and a greatgrandmother, both living in the same house. He distinguishes between them by using the floors on which they live. With a simple understanding of his 94-year-old greatgrandmother's needs he spends time with her listening to her stories, seeing not the elderly lady she is now but the person she has always been. While he loves both elderly ladies, it is his greatgrandmother with whom he feels most empathy. When she dies he finds it difficult to understand, and responds by dropping his identification code from his grandmother's name. His mother encourages him to think of a shooting star as a kiss from Nana Upstairs. Later as an adult he experiences the death of his grandmother and on seeing a shooting star thinks of both grandmothers as being upstairs.
AGE INTEREST LEVEL: I,Lp

72 NOBODY'S PERFECT

Hessell, Jenny
Nelson, Mandy
Hutchinson, 1989, *1 86941 054 8* Hb
Mum has explained all about the terrible things that can happen to careless children, but she has never mentioned that you could die 'just doing nothing'. When another child in the class becomes ill and dies the boy is very angry that this could happen as the child had done nothing wrong. It takes mum a while to explain and to calm his anger and fear. There is conflict between the family and school over the initial explanation.
AGE INTEREST LEVEL: Lp

73 NO TIME FOR GOODBYES: COPING WITH SORROW, ANGER AND INJUSTICE AFTER A TRAGIC DEATH

Lord, Janice Harris

Pedersen, Patricia

Pathfinder, 1988, rev ed *0 934793 11 5* Pb

This is one of the few books which deals with the violent death of parents, children and siblings through murder, hit-and-run accidents etc. The author describes how people react and includes many quotations from people who have suffered such a loss. As the book is American, the section on 'Coping with the criminal justice system' is not relevant to the British context. Most of the chapter on 'Financial Challenges' is relevant to the British situation.

AGE INTEREST LEVEL: A

74 ON CHILDREN AND DEATH

Kubler-Ross, Elisabeth

Macmillan, 1983, *0 02 567110 3* Hb

From an author who has written many books about children and death comes this collection of articles, interviews and diaries. Parents, families, siblings and friends talk about the loss of a child and the long grieving period. Included are poems and stories which have been written by mourning family members. Surrounding these excerpts is simple, straightforward practical and sympathetic advice and support from someone who knows what she is talking about. This is therapautic for those who are sorrowing and helpful for counsellors wanting to know how to help a family mourning the death of a child.

AGE INTEREST LEVEL: A

75 ONE GREEN LEAF

Ure, Jean

Corgi Freeway, 1990, *0 552 52506 5* Pb

Bodley Head, 1987, *0 370 30784 4* Pb

Four teenagers who have gone through school together reach their sixth year and relationships change. David and Abbey pair off and become serious about each other, while Zoot and Robyn remain good friends. Their complacency is shattered when it is found that David has a tumour in his leg and that the leg will have to be amputated. After his return to school the friends help David as he comes to terms with losing his leg, but they slowly realise that he will never recover. David's death is told only in retrospect but is no less alarming. These are four young people faced with a reality and inevitability that forces them to grow up very quickly.

AGE INTEREST LEVEL: S

76 ON MY HONOUR

Bauer, Marion Dane
Pan, 1988, *0 330 30459 3* Pb
Chivers Press, 1989, *0 7451 086 5* LP

Joel's best friend Tony challenges him to swim in the local river. Although warned by his father to stay away, Joel agrees, not wanting Tony to think he is scared. It is not until both boys are in the water that Joel realises Tony can't swim. When Tony disappears Joel tries frantically to find him, and fails. A profound sense of guilt eventually gives Joel the courage to tell the truth about the incident.

AGE INTEREST LEVEL: S

77 A PARCEL OF PATTERNS

Walsh, Jill Paton
Viking Kestrel, 1986, *0 670 80861 X* Hb
Penguin, 1988, *0 14 032627 8* Pb
Chivers Press, 1989, *07451 0926 8* Lp

Death by plague rarely happens now. In this historical novel the details of how the villagers of Eyam in Derbyshire isolated themselves in order to stop the plague spreading are related with care and compassion. The villagers traced the germs to a parcel of patterns sent from London, and endeavoured to look after those afflicted while trying to stop friends and relatives from entering the village. Although most of the characters are imaginary, the actual story is recorded, and it is the starkness of the truth which affects the reader. Woven into the framework of the story are attitudes and responses to the horrors of this illness and the almost inevitable death it brought. They are clearly indicative of thoughts and social mores at the time the incident happened.

AGE INTEREST LEVEL: S

78 PHOENIX RISING OR HOW TO SURVIVE YOUR LIFE

Grant, Cynthia

Collins Lions, 1991, *0 0 673732 3* Pb

Jessie's older sister Helen has died of cancer and she is finding it very hard to understand. Though her parents and brother try to help she becomes more and more withdrawn. Part of the story is told through extracts from Helen's diary, which Jessie has found. By reading how Helen has comes to terms with her impending death and getting to know Helen's boyfriend she slowly comes to accept her grief.

AGE INTEREST LEVEL: S

79 RED SKY IN THE MORNING

Laird, Elizabeth

Heinemann, 1988, *0 434 94714 8* Hb

Heinemann Education, 1990, *0435 12355* 6 Hb

Pan, 1989, *0 330 30890 4* Pb

Anna is twelve when her baby brother Ben is born. Ben's arrival puts a strain on the family as he suffers from hydrocephalus and needs special care. Gradually Anna overcomes her initial reticence at having a brother with special needs and begins telling her friends about Ben. She comes to love him and to see him as an individual with his own personality. His tragic death at the age of two is hard for the family to accept.

AGE INTEREST LEVEL: S

80 REMEMBERING GRANDAD: FACING UP TO DEATH

Padoan, Gianni

Collini, Emanuela

Child's Play (International), 1987, *0 85953 311* 5 Hb

Originally published in Italy, this picture book tells the story of James whose grandfather has just died. With help from his friends Joe and Gwen he remembers the good times they had together. Though he is sad at not having Grandad to play with in person, he realises that in his memory Grandad will always be with him. By discussing how he feels with his friends he is also helping them to understand death and grieving.

AGE INTEREST LEVEL: I,Lp,Up

81 REMEMBERING MUM

Perkins, Ginny & Morris, Leon
A & C Black, 1991, *0 7136 3381* 6 Hb
Sam and Eddy's mum has died and they miss her a lot, but they remember her in different ways — taking flowers to the cemetery, looking at photographs with dad, talking about the things they did together, planting a special garden at school. The three of them allowed A&C Black to photograph them doing these things together, talking about Mandy and thinking of the past. This is a very personal book which shows clearly the process of bereavement within a family unit.
AGE INTEREST LEVEL: I,Lp,Up

82 ROSE BLANCHE

McEwan, Ian
Innocenti, Roberto
Jonathan Cape, 1985, *0 224 02841 3* Hb
A beautifully illustrated poignant story of a young girl in war-torn Europe who watches as her Jewish friends and neighbours are taken away. She follows the death-laden trucks to the forest and sees the misery and hopelessness of those who are forceably imprisoned. Rose Blanche is killed, shot by soldiers who might have been the enemy, or might have been allies.
AGE INTEREST LEVEL: Up,S

83 RUN, RUN, AS FAST AS YOU CAN

Osborne, Mary Pope
Patrick Hardy, 1983, *0 7444 0021 X* Hb
Moving to a new town, Hallie wants to be accepted by the popular girls in her class, but this does not happen. She finds comfort in playing with her younger brother, but when he becomes ill with cancer she is devastated. Part of the problem lies in the fact that her parents won't tell her what's happening to Mickey and she feels angry and bewildered at their exclusion. A neighbour who she considered a 'plain Jane' turns out to be a great help and support. The story portrays very vividly the importance of parents talking to children about life threatening diseases and death.
AGE INTEREST LEVEL: S

84 SAY GOODNIGHT, GRACIE

Reece Deaver, Julie
Macmillan, 1988, *0 333 47608 5* Hb
Macmillan, 1989, *0 333 47609 3* Pb

Jimmy and Morgan grew up together, sharing their joys and triumphs, especially Jimmy's determination to be a professional dancer. When Jimmy is killed by a hit-and-run driver Morgan needs professional help in overcoming her anger. She begins to fail at school and to lose her sense of identity. After some counselling sessions Morgan understands that she must allow Jimmy to die in her mind, while still remembering him, in order to continue her own life.

AGE INTEREST LEVEL: S

85 SAYING GOOD-BYE TO GRANDMA

Thomas, Jane Resh
Sewall, Marcia
Clarion Books, 1988, *0 8919 654 4* Hb

When Suzie's grandma dies, she goes back with her parents to the small town where her mother grew up to attend Grandma's funeral. At seven years of age Suzie has never been to a funeral before. She is curious about what is to happen but also fearful. With help from her family and relatives she gets caught up in the rituals of death and finds that as well as sadness there is also happiness in remembrance.

AGE INTEREST LEVEL: I,Lp,Up

86 SO LONG AT THE FAIR

Irwin, Hadley
Viking Kestrel, 1990, *0 670 82988 9* Pb
Penguin, 1991, *0 14 034232 7* Pb

Suicide is always tragic, as is any death, but when there seems no reason it is difficult to understand. Joel cannot believe that Ashley would kill herself, and in trying to divorce himself from the horror of his memories he wanders into working at a fairground. He remembers their childhood, the family outings, growing up, their close relationship, but cannot come to terms with the fact that she didn't share her unhappiness with him. Both young people had loving families, at least on the surface, and money to do what they wanted, and yet the complexity of suicide evades Joel's understanding. It takes a long time and a lot of heart searching

before Joel can even begin to see Ashley's side of the story and his grieving can begin.
AGE INTEREST LEVEL: S

87 SOME OF THE PIECES

Madenski, Melisa
Ray, Dorothy Kogan
Little Brown, 1991, *0 316 54324 1* Hb
Dylan lost his father a year previously, but his mum, younger sister and he always talk about him. They share the memories of the things they did together and though at times they hurt, gradually these thoughts of Dad make them smile. Dad was cremated and over a period of time they scatter the ashes in all the places Dad loved and where they had good times with him.
AGE INTEREST LEVEL: Up

88 SOMEONE SPECIAL HAS DIED

St. Christopher's Hospice
Crossland, Caroline
St. Christopher's Hospice, 1989, Pb
51–59 Lawrie Park Road
London SE26 6DZ Pam
This simple eight page introduction to death explains how a child may feel and encourages families to talk about the dead person. One helpful suggestion is to assist the child to make a scrapbook of memories.
AGE INTEREST LEVEL: A

89 A SOUND OF CHARIOTS

Hunter, Mollie
Collins Lions, 1988, *0 00 672092 7* Pb
Magna, 1987, *1 85057 183 X* Hb,Lp
Magna, 1987, *1 85057 184 8* Pb,Lp
Set in Scotland just after the First World War, this is the story of Bridie McShane and the special relationship she has with her father. His death leaves her disconsolate and very aware of the frailty of human life. Through the characteristics she has inherited from him — fighting spirit, honesty, love of books — she comes to terms with her loss.
AGE INTEREST LEVEL: S

90 A SPECIAL SCAR: THE EXPERIENCE OF PEOPLE BEREAVED BY SUICIDE

Wertheimer, Alison
Routledge, 1991, *0 415 01762 9* Hb
Routledge, 1991, *0 415 01763 7* Pb

This title looks in detail at the stigma surrounding suicide, and offers practical help for relatives and friends of people who have taken their own life, and also those who have survived a suicide attempt. Fifty bereaved people tell their own stories, showing us that by not hiding the truth from themselves and others, they have been able to learn to live with suicide. These articles are used as examples throughout the various chapters — Meeting the Survivors, Looking Back, Why did it Happen?, The Inquest, The Funeral, Facing the World, Looking for Support.

AGE INTEREST LEVEL: A

91 A STAR FOR THE LATECOMER

Zindel, Paul and Zindel, Bonnie
Lions, 1981, *0 00 671787 X* Pb
Red Fox, 1991, *0 09 987200 5* Pb

Brooke's mother had always been ambitious for her, insisting that the girl become a straight A student, be the best dancer, have a career on stage, and never accept defeat. As she grew up Brooke accepted this, but when her mother develops cancer Brooke becomes increasingly independent and begins to see herself as an entity, someone capable of living her own life. Brooke struggles to come to terms with her mother's terminal illness, her father's distress and her own changing views. The death of the parent is a tragedy but also the means through which Brooke can begin to live life on her own terms.

AGE INTEREST LEVEL: S

92 SUICIDE AND ATTEMPTED SUICIDE AMONG CHILDREN AND ADOLESCENTS

Hawton, Keith
Sage, 1986, *0 8039 2522 0* Hb
Sage, 1986, *0 8039 2523 9* Pb

Suicidal behaviour by children or adolescents understandably evokes dramatic emotional responses in most people, many of whom cannot comprehend how a young person can find life so awful that they wish to end it or put it seriously at risk. The book gives a straightforward account of what is known about suicidal behaviour among young people which will enable those working with children to begin to formulate plans for its management and hopefully prevention. Facts and figures are given for Australia, UK, USA and other countries where there has been an increase in this behaviour.

AGE INTEREST LEVEL: A

93 A SUMMER TO DIE

Lowry, Lois

Collins Lion, 1990, *0 00 673598 3* Pb

Meg is the serious one, hardworking but uninspired, while Molly is pretty, calm and straightforward. One summer after the family moves to the country Molly becomes ill with constant nose bleeds. When she returns home from hospital, both Molly and Meg know it is for the last time. Unfortunately for the family Molly dies in hospital after a long drawn out illness, but Meg is able to understand that living and dying are part of the pattern of days. She can mourn Molly but also look forward to her own life.

AGE INTEREST LEVEL: S

94 TALKING ABOUT BEREAVEMENT

Richardson, Rosamond (ed)

Optima, 1991, *0 356 20236 4* Pb

Experiences of death and bereavement are described by fifteen families. Losses include a baby at birth, an eighteen-year-old son, a stepbrother, a two-year-old daughter, parents. All the contributors talk openly about their feelings and reactions — the symptoms of grief — denial, anger and sadness, how they coped and in what ways. By sharing their stories we can come to understand our own feelings about bereavement.

AGE INTEREST LEVEL: A

95 TALKING ABOUT GRIEF: FOUR SEMINARS

Casdagli, Penny

Neti Neti Theatre Co, 1991, *0 9514242 1 4* Pb

These four seminar papers explore the ways grief affects young people and complement the play 'Grief' (see entry 48). The four seminars are: How To Talk about Death with Young People, Helping Young People

with the grieving Process, Young People Talk about Loss and Change and How Grief Affects Young People's Behaviour. There are also contributions from professionals in the field and writings from young people themselves.
AGE INTEREST LEVEL: A

96 A TASTE OF BLACKBERRIES

Smith, Doris Buchanan
Binch, Caroline
Heinemann, 1986, *0 434 93015* 6 Hb
Puffin, 1987, *0 14 032020* 2 Pb
Macmillan Educ., 1989, *0 333 46224* 6 Pb
Windrush, 1990, *1 85089 820 0* Lp
Jamie played the fool and tried to make everyone notice him. When he was stung by angry bees his friends didn't bother with his display of exaggerated hurt. The bee stings killed Jamie, and his friends face grief, remorse and anger before coming to terms with the accident. The portrayal of the two mothers is particularly good, as is the children's reluctance to visit Jamie's house after his death.
AGE INTEREST LEVEL: Lp,Up

97 THE TENTH GOOD THING ABOUT BARNEY

Viorst, Judith
Collins, 1973, *0 00 195821* 6 Hb
Barney the family cat dies, and they are desolate, especially the children. After they have buried him in the garden, mum suggests that they remember all the good things about Barney so that their memories are happy. There is no difficulty with the first few, but as the list gets longer the children have to think harder. The tenth good thing shows how matter-of-fact children can be about death — Barney is helping the flowers to grow.
AGE INTEREST LEVEL: 1 Lp

98 THUNDERWITH

Hathorn, Libby
Heinemann, 1990, *0 434 94204* 9 Hb
Mammoth, 1991, *0 7497 0423* 3 Pb
After the death of her mother, Lara goes to live with the father she never

knew, his new wife and their four children. She finds it strange living in the country after being used to the city. Her new family and her fellow pupils at school do not like her and she feels very isolated. Through her friendship with a local storyteller she starts to talk about her grief at losing her mother and about her new family. Naturally, there are two sides to every story and she comes to terms with the fact that her father's new family are scared of her, because they think she might take him away. A school bully brings the children together and helps them to realize that they need each other.

AGE INTEREST LEVEL: S

99 A TIDE FLOWING

Phipson, Joan

Methuen, 1981, *0 416 21470 3* Hb

Mark and his mother leave home and a broken marriage to start a new life in a new area. They go sailing with friends and Mark's mother goes overboard and is drowned. Although he attempts to settle with his grandparents, Mark never really comes to terms with his mother's death and years later begins to talk of it to a girl whose life he has saved. The later death of the girl in some way frees Mark to understand the tension within his family and to think about the reason for his mother's death. A strongly written novel for teenagers which asks questions about suicide, family loyalty, communication and fate.

AGE INTEREST LEVEL: S

100 TIGGER AND FRIENDS

Hamley, Dennis

Rutherford, Meg

Andre Deutsch, 1989, *0 233 98213 2* Hb

Collins, 1990, *0 00 663507 5* Pb

Tigger is used to being the only cat in the house and is very annoyed when a new kitten, Thomas, arrives. Eventually they become friends and spend many happy years together. Thomas's death leaves Tigger devastated, but he is even more upset when another new kitten arrives. Then he remembered how he felt when Thomas first came and the good times they had, and he comes to accept Thomas's death and the new cat.

AGE INTEREST LEVEL: I,Lp

101 TO HELL WITH DYING

Walker, Alice
Deeter, Catherine
Hodder and Stoughton, 1988, *0 340 43022 2* Hb
Hodder and Stoughton, 1991, *0 340 53232 7* Pb

Mr Sweet was well known in his local community as 'an alcoholic, a diabetic and a guitar player'. He also has a habit of 'dying' on a regular basis. The narrator of this story is the un-named girl who, throughout her life has been a part of Mr Sweet's 'revivals', when he pretended that only the presence of children could bring him back to life. Here she remembers those times with sadness and humour, having just taken part in the last 'revival', the one from which Mr Sweet did not recover. The old man gave himself to the community around him, he was part of living and growing. Mr Sweet is remembered for his ability to soothe and comfort, for his music and his listening skills, not for his drinking or morbidity.

AGE INTEREST LEVEL: Up,S

102 TWO WEEKS WITH THE QUEEN

Gleitzman, Morris
Blackie, 1989, *0 216 92761 7* Hb
Pan Books, 1990, *0 330 31376 2* Pb

When Colin is told that his brother Luke has cancer his feelings are mixed. Then to be told he is being shipped off to England while his brother is ill intensifies the feeling — that he is not wanted. Once in England Colin decides that as the doctors don't seem able to cure Luke the next best person is the Queen, and he makes up his mind to see her. This, however, proves very difficult, and along the way Colin meets and makes friends with a young man whose companion is dying of AIDS. It is watching Ted grieve that helps Colin understand why he must insist on going home to be with Luke. This is not a happy story, although it does have humorous moments. But it tackles head on the agonising decision of telling a child about terminal illness, and of helping a child to understand a little the tragedy of AIDS.

AGE INTEREST LEVEL: Up,S

103 UNDERSTANDING DYING, DEATH, & BEREAVEMENT

Leming, Michael R. & Dickinson, George E.
Holt Rinehart & Winston, 1990, 2nd ed. *0 03 028377 9* Hb
This publication looks in detail at death in the USA and how society copes with it. Chapters deal with understanding the social meanings of death and dying; religion and death attitudes; the hospice approach; euthanasia and biomedical issues; children and death; the history of bereavement and burial practices in America. Though it is American, there are ideas which could be transferred to the British situation. It is also useful in showing how death and bereavement are dealt with in another country.
AGE INTEREST LEVEL: A

104 THE VERY BEST OF FRIENDS

Wild, Margaret
Vivas, Julie
Bodley Head, 1990, *0 370 31435 2* Hb
Jessie and James live on a farm with a vast assortment of animals, including a cat named William whom Jessie can't abide. William avoids annoying Jessie and tries to be as helpful as possible, but to no avail. When James dies suddenly, it is William who tries desperately to help, but finds himself banished to the farmyard. He becomes bad tempered and wild, scratching Jessie one morning when she puts out the food. Jessie begins to realise how mean she has been to the cat and welcomes him into the house again, seeing him as a part of James she can still share.
AGE INTEREST LEVEL: Lp

105 WATER BUGS AND DRAGONFLIES: EXPLAINING DEATH TO CHILDREN

Stickney, Doris
Oritz, Gloria
Mowbray, 1989, *0 264 66904 5* Pb
The author has used the waterbug's life under water, and its emergence into the world above the water as a dragonfly, as an analogy for human life on earth and life after death. The book is very much written from the

Christian point of view with additional material in the way of prayers and quotations from the Bible.
AGE INTEREST LEVEL: I,Lp

106 WE, THE HAUNTED

Johnson, Pete
Collins Lions Tracks, 1989, *0 00 673160 0* Pb
Caro and Paul meet, fall in love and become inseparable. Paul goes off on holiday with his family and is drowned in a boating accident. Caro is inconsolable and through her grief will not let Paul go. She imagines Paul has come back. Paul's best friend Dean tells most of the story as he sees Caro becoming obsessed with Paul's memory. Though she is always rude to him he realises that unless she accepts Paul's death and comes to terms with it she will become mentally ill.
AGE INTEREST LEVEL: S

107 WHAT'S UP MATE?

Bales, Helen
Stanish, Paul
Hodder and Stoughton, 1987, *0 340 35983 8* Hb
This was specially written for children by a parent whose young son died of leukemia. She has used simple medical terms to explain the various treatments a child might undergo, and talks about being in hospital, the possible effects of treatment, and the uneasiness of Billy as he undergoes spinal taps and scans. Couched in easily readable language the book reassures while at the same time honestly states the problems of cancer. The book ends when Billy goes home after his first period of treatment. This should not be given to a child to read alone, but should be shared with an adult and discussed calmly.
AGE INTEREST LEVEL: Lp,Up

108 WHEN A BABY DIES: THE EXPERIENCE OF LATE MISCARRIAGE, STILLBIRTH AND NEONATAL DEATH

Kohner, Nancy and Henley, Alix
Pandora, 1991, *0 04 440566 9* Pb
This book was produced in co-operation with SANDS — the Stillbirth and Neonatal Death Society. Parents talk about the death of their child,

their experiences in hospital, grief and grieving, and pregnancy following an infant death. Medical causes of still birth and neonatal deaths are explained. The book is mainly for parents, but will also be useful for professionals in the field as it contains a chapter on good professional practice. A list of helpful organisations and charities is included.

AGE INTEREST LEVEL: A

109 WHEN DAD DIED

Hollins, Sheila & Sireling, Lester
Webb, Elizabeth
St. Georges Hospital Medical School, 1989, 1 85183 019 7 Pb

WHEN MUM DIED 1 85183 020 0 Pb

Cranmer Terrace
Tooting
London SW17 0RE

These books are identical except for the actual funeral. Dad's funeral is a cremation, while Mum's is a burial. They give a straightforward account of a death in the family. The approach is very simple and honest with a two page spread for each separate topic. There is a maximum of six lines of text on the left page and a colour picture on the right page which mirrors the text. The books can be used with a variety of ages, and are also very good for use with intellectually handicapped young adults.

AGE INTEREST LEVEL: Lp, Up, S, A

110 WHEN UNCLE BOB DIED

Althea
Kopper, Lisa
Dinosaur, 1988, *0 85122 727* 9 Pb

A simple text with illustrations on each page. Beginning with a butterfly, a mother explains to her young child that you don't recover from death; it isn't an illness. The death of his Uncle Bob makes the child angry, and he wishes his parents had let him attend the funeral. The text explains how some people are buried after death and others cremated, touches on the process of grieving, and explains that having fun after a death is all right too. The child worries when his own father is ill that he will die, but is reassured by his mother. The family share their grief and remember Uncle Bob through family relationships and memories.

AGE INTEREST LEVEL: I,Lp

111 WHY DID GRANDMA DIE?

Madler, Trudy

Connelly, Gwen

Blackwell Raintree, 1981, *0 86256 001 2* Hb

Helen and her grandmother do many things together and she is very upset when her gran dies. She doesn't understand why it had to happen. Her parents explain about old age and that everybody has a certain time to live. Though the body is dead they leave many things behind and Helen thinks of all the things that Gran has taught her to do.

AGE INTEREST LEVEL: Lp,Up

112 WILL MY RABBIT GO TO HEAVEN? AND OTHER QUESTIONS CHILDREN ASK

Hughes, Jerimie

Geary, Bob

Lion, 1988, rev ed *0 7459 1221 4* Pb

A light-hearted look at all those questions children ask at one time or the other, and quite often at inappropriate moments! There are chapters on God, death and suffering, heaven and the other place, the world, sex, and family life. The book does not set out to give the definitive answer, but it may help you out of an embarrassing moment and also give you a laugh at some of the comments that children make.

AGE INTEREST LEVEL: Up,S

113 YOUR FRIEND, REBECCA

Hoy, Linda

Bodley Head, 1981, *0 370 30418 7* Pb

Beaver Books, 1983, *0 09 031280 8* Pb

Rebecca and her father both mourn the loss of a mother and wife, but are unable to express their grief to each other. Rebecca's disquiet and frustration is expressed in her behaviour at school, while her father tries to recapture his youth. It is through drama and the reading of King Lear that Rebecca is able to admit her fears to herself, and gradually begin to communicate with her father until they can share their grief.

AGE INTEREST LEVEL: S

KEYWORD INDEX

In order to simplify the use of this handbook all entries are arranged alphabetically by title in the main section, with every entry being given an individual number. This index allows the user to find a specific topic and go direct to the given numbered entries.

ACCIDENTAL DEATH:	allergy 96
	drowning 8, 43, 63, 76, 99, 106
	road 4, 19, 30, 37, 48, 54, 70, 84
	other 38, 57
BIBLIOGRAPHIES:	7, 20
COUNSELLING:	3, 9, 10, 14, 16, 18, 24, 32, 41, 44, 49, 50, 53, 60, 62, 64, 74, 90, 92, 95, 103, 108
DEATH OF A:	child 1, 8, 9, 11, 24, 36, 38, 39, 43, 48, 51, 54, 61, 65, 72, 76, 79, 82, 83, 93, 96, 107, 108
	friend 6, 8, 12, 43, 51, 54, 56, 72, 75, 76, 84, 86, 96, 101, 106
	grandparent 2, 27, 45, 46, 67, 71, 80, 85, 111
	husband/wife 13, 89, 104, 113
	other relative 29,110
	parent 13, 19, 28, 52, 58, 59, 63, 66, 81, 87, 89, 91, 98, 99, 104, 109, 113
	pet 30, 35, 37, 42, 47, 55, 97, 100
	sibling 4, 15, 24, 48, 57, 61, 65, 69, 70, 78, 79, 83, 93
DEATH PRACTICES:	103
	burial 40, 109
	cremation 109
	religious observances 22, 23, 25, 31
EXPLAINING DEATH:	3, 5, 17, 21, 24, 26, 33, 43, 47, 49, 54, 56, 67, 72, 74, 85, 88, 105, 109, 110, 111, 112
HOSPICE/MEDICAL CARE:	2, 10, 36, 41, 53, 62, 64, 107
OLD AGE:	12, 27, 71, 101, 111
SUICIDE:	15, 51, 69, 86, 90, 92
TERMINAL ILLNESS:	AIDS 102
	Anorexia nervosa 11
	cancer (including leukemia) 2, 6, 29, 36, 66, 75, 78, 83, 91, 93, 98, 102, 107
	heart disease 13, 65, 109

other 77, 79
VIOLENT DEATH: 73
disaster 77
kidnapping 1
war or civil disturbance 39, 58, 82, 89

AUTHOR INDEX

Numbers refer to the individual entry numbers not page numbers

ALEXANDER, Sue 61
ALIKI 35
ALTHEA 110
BALES, Helen 107
BARNETT, Vida 31
BAUER, Marion Dane 76
BAUM, J D 62
BERNSTEIN, Joanne 7
BRIGHTON, Catherine 12
BUCKMAN, Dr Robert 53
BURNINGHAM, John 45
CASDAGLI, Penny 48, 95
CORMIER, Robert 1
CRUTCHER, Chris 15
COHN, Janice 54
DAY, David 4
DePAOLA, Tomie 71
DUNBAR, Maureen 11
DYREGROV, Atle 49
EGGER, Bettina 67
FOSTER, Suzanne 9
GLEITZMAN, Morris 102
GODDEN, Rumer 27
GOULD, Deborah 46
GRANT, Cynthia 78
GREEN, Wendy 47
HAMLEY, Dennis 100
HARLEY, Rex 51
HATHORN, Libby 98
HAWTON, Keith 92
HESSELL, Jenny 72
HILL, Susan 34
HOLLINS, Sheila 109
HORN, Sandra 16
HOWKER, Janni 57
HOY, Linda 113
HUGHES, Jeremie 112
HUNTER, Mollie 89
IRWIN, Hadley 86
JOHNSON, Pete 106
JUDD, Dorothy 41
KALDHOL, Marit 43
KELLER, Holly 42
KEY, Sarah 38
KOHNER, Nancy 108
KREMENTZ, Jill 52
KUBLER-ROSS, Elisabeth 64, 74
LAIRD, Elizabeth 79
LAMERTON, Richard 10
LEE, Virginia 65
LEMING, Michael 103
LEVINE, Stephen 68
LITTLE, Jean 66
LLOYD, Carole 13
LORD, Janice Harris 73
LOWRY, Lois 93
McEWAN, Ian 82
MADENSKI, Melissa 87
MADLER, Trudy 111
MAHY, Margaret 69
MAYLED, Jon 22
MAZER, Norma Fox 2
MELLONIE, Bryan 5
MENTAL HEALTH MEDIA COUNCIL 20
MUSTY, Erica 14, 23
NAUGHTON, Jim 70
NYSTROM, Carolyn 29
OSBORNE, Mary Pope 83
PADOAN, Gianni 80
PARR, Letitia 37
PATERSON, Katherine 8

PERKINS, Ginny 81
PHILPOT, Terry 60
PHIPSON, Joan 99
PICTORIAL CHARTS
EDUCATIONAL TRUST 25
RAAB, Dr Robert 17
RAPHAEL, Beverley 3
REECE DEAVER, Julie 84
RICHARDSON, Rosamond 94
RICHTER, Hans Peter 39
ST CHRISTOPHER'S HOSPICE 88
SAUNDERS, Pete 21
SMITH, Doris Buchanan 96
SMITH, Linda 26
SNELL, Nigel 30
STEDEFORD, Averil 32
STICKNEY, Doris 105
STILES, Norman 56
STILZ, Carol Curtis 59
STUART, Alexander 36
TALBERT, Marc 19
TATELBAUM, Judy 18
THOMAS, Jane Resh 85
URE, Jean 75
VIORST, Judith 97
WADDELL, Martin 63
WALKER, Alice 101
WALLBANK, Susan 33
WALSH, Jill Paton 77
WALTER, Dr Tony 40
WARD, Barbara 44
WELLS, Rosemary 50
WERTHEIMER, Alison 90
WESTALL, Robert 58
WILD, Margaret 104
WILHELM, Hans 55
WILKINSON, Tessa 24
WRIGHT, Gilli 28
ZINDEL, Paul 6, 91

ORGANISATIONS AND THEIR ADDRESSES

These organisations offer help and advice to those caring for children who are suffering from a life-threatening condition, and people who have been bereaved and are grieving. Most organisations have printed leaflets available. When writing for information it is best to enclose a large stamped self-addressed envelope.

ACTION FOR SICK CHILDREN, (NAWCH)
Argyle House, 29–31 Euston Road, London NW1. Tel: 071 833 2041

Works for the welfare of children in hospital.

ACT
Institute of Child Health, Royal Hospital for Sick Children, St Michael's Hill, Bristol BS2 8BJ. Tel: 0272 22 1556

Help for families whose children have life-threatening and terminal conditions.

BACUP
121–123 Charterhouse Street, London EC1M 6AA. Tel: 071 608 1661

For information on cancer and caring for a patient with cancer.

BEREAVED PARENTS HELPLINE
6 Cannons Gate, Harlow, Essex. Tel: 0279 41 2745

BRITISH ASSOCIATION FOR COUNSELLING
37a Sheep Street, Rugby, Warwickshire CV21 3BX. Tel: 0788 57 8328

Will give advice, support and counselling.

CANCER RELIEF MACMILLAN FUND
Anchor House, 15–19 Britten Street, London SW3 3TZ. Tel: 071 351 7811

Gives advice and information on home and hospice care.

CANCER AND LEUKEMIA IN CHILDHOOD TRUST (CLIC)
CLIC House, 11–12 Freemantle Square, Cotham Bristol, Avon BS6 5TL. Tel: 0272 24 4333

Support, information advice for sufferers and their families.

THE COMPASSIONATE FRIENDS
Mrs Anne Pocock, 6 Denmark Street, Bristol BS1 5DQ. Tel: 0272 29 2778

An international organisation of bereaved parents offering friendship and support — local groups in some areas.

COT DEATH RESEARCH AND SUPPORT GROUP FOR BEREAVED PARENTS
8a Alexandra Parade, Weston-Super-Mare, Avon BS23 1TQ. Tel: 0836 21 9010, 0934 41 3333

Gives counselling and counselling training.

CRUSE
Cruse House, 126 Sheen Road, Richmond, Surrey TW9 1UR. Tel: 081 940 4818

Provides suppport and help for all bereaved persons, especially siblings.

DEPARTMENT OF SOCIAL SECURITY
Leaflets Unit, PO Box 21, Stanmore, Middlesex HA7 1AY.

Provides various guides.

FOUNDATION FOR THE STUDY OF INFANT DEATHS
15 Belgrave Square, London SW1X 8PS.

Offers support and help to parents whose children have died from cot deaths.

GOOD GRIEF
Good Grief, 19 Bawtree Road, Uxbridge, Middlesex UB8 1PT.

Runs courses on counselling and learning about bereavement. Aimed at parents, teachers, carers and children.

HOSPICE INFORMATION SERVICE
(see St Christopher's Hospice entry.)

JEWISH BEREAVEMENT COUNSELLING SERVICE
Mrs June Epstein, Co-Ordinator, 1 Cyprus Gardens, London N3 1SP. Tel: 081 349 0839 (answering machine) 071 387 4300 ext. 227 (office hours only)

Covers the London area only.

LONDON BEREAVEMENT PROJECTS CO-ORDINATING GROUP
68 Chalton Street, London NW1 1JR. Tel: 071 388 0241

NATIONAL ASSOCIATION OF BEREAVEMENT SERVICES
20 Norton Folgate, Bishopsgate, London E1 6DB. Tel: 071 247 1080

Umbrella organisation for all bereavement organisations.

NATIONAL ASSOCIATION FOR HOSPITAL PLAY STAFF
Thomas Coram Foundation for Children, 40 Brunswick Square, London WC1. Tel: 071 278 2424

NATIONAL CHILDREN'S BUREAU
8 Wakely Street, London EC1V 7QE. Tel: 071 278 9441

THE NATIONAL SOCIETY (CHURCH OF ENGLAND) FOR PROMOTING RELIGIOUS EDUCATION
Church House, Great Smith Street, London SW1P 3NZ. Tel: 071 222 1672

NATURAL DEATH CENTRE
20 Heber Road, Cricklewood, London NW2 6AA Tel: 081 208 2853

Provides advice to the dying and their families through a national network of support groups.

PARENTS OF MURDERED CHILDREN SUPPORT GROUP
10 Eastern Avenue, Prittewell, Southend on Sea, Essex SS2 5QU. Tel: 0702 68510

An organisation linked to Compassionate Friends.

ROYAL SOCIETY FOR MENTALLY HANDICAPPED CHILDREN AND ADULTS (MENCAP)
117–123 Golden Lane, London EC1 0RF. Tel: 071 253 9433

ST CHRISTOPHER'S HOSPICE
Halley Stewart Library, 51–59 Lawrie Park Road, Sydenham, London SE26 6DZ. Tel: 081 778 9252

The library contains a specialised, multidisciplinary collection of literature on care of the terminally ill, and bereavement.

SAMARITANS
Head Office, 10 The Grove, Slough, Berkshire SL1 1QP. Tel: 0753 53 2713

SANDS
28 Portland Place, London W1N 4DE. Tel: 071 436 5881

Stillbirth and Neonatal Death. There are self-help groups nation-wide.

TERRENCE HIGGINS TRUST
52–54 Grays Inn Road, London WC1X 8JU. Tel: 071 831 0330

For all information on caring for people with AIDS.

TWINS BEREAVEMENT SUPPORT GROUP
Mrs S Payne, 59 Sunnyside, Worksop, Nottinghamshire S81 7LN.

Gives support to families who have lost a twin or twins.

YAD B YAD (HAND IN HAND)
8 Grove Avenue, London N10 2AR.

A resource centre for parents and teachers for use mainly by the Jewish community.